PRESENTED TO

_____

FROM

_____

MONEY BASIC$

FOR

EVERYDAY PEOPLE

FIVE SIMPLE STEPS TO FINANCIAL FREEDOM

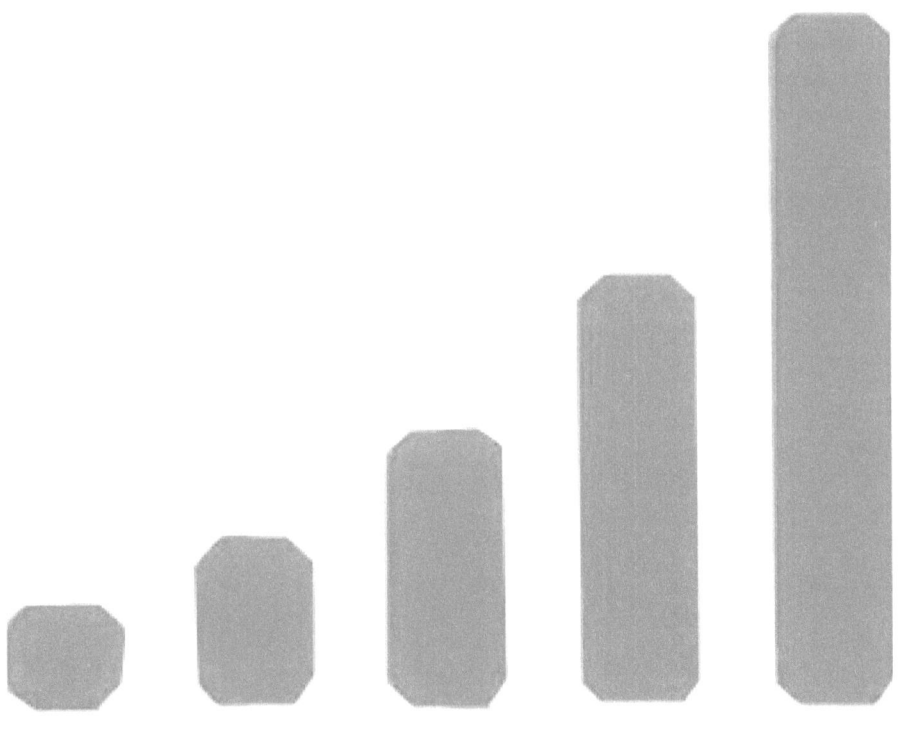

K. C. HOBBS

To order additional copies of this book, contact:
Xlibris Corporation
1-888-795-4274
www.Xlibris.com
Orders@Xlibris.com
70235

CONTENTS

ACKNOWLEDGEMENTS

This book is dedicated to my loving and supportive wife Kelly who is my best friend and true love of my life. With her computer skills she turned my thoughts into print and made this book a reality.

To my parents Kemp and Mary Hobbs who raised me to live by the "Golden Rule" and for always being there for me.

To Mr. Tim Bradshaw for approaching me and sharing the basics of finance.

To Mr. Art Williams whose hard work in building a company that has helped so many thousands of consumers learn about money basics.

To Zyra Myrrh who contacted me to help self publish my book.

To Claire Dael for the work she did to make this special book possible.

To Ruth Gonzaga and her team for their patience and diligence in the completion of my book.

To my publisher Xlibris Publishing for the professional way this book was printed.

INTRODUCTION

In our working lifetime we all earn small fortunes. Then why is it that many Americans retire in poverty? I believe it is a lack of understanding of the basics of money. We all know we need to save for various things, but somehow it is just easier to use a credit card or get a loan. In these few pages hopefully you will grasp a few key ideas that can enrich you and your families lives. My goal in writing this book is to give you a few broad strokes of money basics to use towards the bigger picture of giving you financial freedom.

We are in school 12 years or more and learn very little during that time about money. For 6 years I studied Algebra and Geometry, but not even one course about Money Management! Which subject would be more important in your view? A 1997 survey of high school students were asked questions about money, the average score was an "F" and only 5% scored a "C" or above. Is this the future for our children?

We graduate and then we go out and begin our 30-40 year careers. Out in the workplace we have to fend for ourselves in learning the do's and don'ts when it comes to money matters. When I began working those many years ago flipping hamburgers at a well-known burger chain and getting my first paycheck it was an incredible feeling. Having a few dollars to get what I wanted and enjoy the American Dream, if even in a very small degree was WONDERFUL. Then I realized I didn't know what to do with those hard-earned dollars. Where should I put them? Well I did like most of us and opened a bank savings account. After many paychecks it grew very little, because I had no plan or idea in mind for my money. When I went by the bank to cash my check, I might put some money in my savings account if I had my savings book handy. I usually didn't have it with me, so my money went into my wallet where I spent every last dollar. Does that sound familiar? I'm sure that is the way most of us have done it in the past. If I had known the concepts that are in these chapters then, I would have had a true vision and plan for the money I had earned.

I have often wondered why do they give senior citizen discounts? After working for 30-40 years and earning thousands of dollars, the seniors should all be wealthy. It is the young person in college trying to get an education or the young couple trying to raise a family that could use the discount. Let me explain with a few comparisons:

RETIRED COUPLE	YOUNG COUPLE OR PERSON
No Children at home	Small children at home
Has earned thousands in 30-40 years	Just starting their careers
Paid off mortgage	Buying their first house
Less need for life insurance	Needs the most life insurance
Should have retirement savings	Just starting their savings
Smaller grocery bill	Usually a large grocery bill
Less taxes	Pay the tax burden

Can you see what I mean, it is the young people of this country that could use a discount? I hope you can begin to see the purpose of this book. Helping you to understand just the basics will make such a tremendous difference and maybe you can say NO THANKS to the senior discounts.

In writing this book I have tried to condense the information down into just FIVE SIMPLE STEPS that you must understand and practice. These five steps will be an easy reference point for you to reflect back on and refresh your memory. There are so many topics that deal with finance that it can be so overwhelming to all of us. That is the main reason for only having five steps, to make it easy for you to learn. Just as you know your A, B, C's, financial basics can be easily learned, too. Look for these steps at the end of five of the chapters and also in the back of the book.

One more thought before we dive in. Please pay particular attention to the information in Chapter 2. It contains one of the most important financial keys in the entire book. Hopefully you will nod your head and get the big picture that there is such a need in America today for MONEY BASIC$ for EVERYDAY PEOPLE.

CHAPTER ONE

GET STARTED TODAY

What is under your sofa cushions, on your dresser or in your car's ashtray? It could be the beginning of your retirement fund. In these pages, you will find out how you could possibly retire on your **loose change**! Amazing as it may seem, it is a proven fact that even saving small amounts can add up to great riches over time.

Many people face a big hurdle in building their riches. That hurdle is procrastination. Americans are very good at procrastinating, especially when it comes to saving money. That unique ability to postpone starting long-term savings seems to have become the American way. Hopefully as you read more you will stop putting off starting and learn to make your money work for you.

The days seem to fly by as you get older. I look back at high school and it feels like yesterday, not many years ago. Since time flies, you need to begin saving today. No one can afford to put off another day or another year something as urgent as their financial future. Retirement may seem a lifetime away, but it will be here before you know it. Do you want to be able to travel and enjoy your later years or do you want to struggle to pay your bills? I believe most of us want to enjoy our leisure years not having to depend solely on a social security check. Start today providing for those golden years.

A FORTUNE IN EARNINGS

Over the course of a person's career, they will earn a small fortune. Have you ever thought about how much you actually earn over those working years? Check out this example:

$20,000 annual earnings X 40 years = $800,000
$30,000 annual earnings X 40 years = $1,200,000
$40,000 annual earnings X 40 years = $1,600,000

Those are some incredible figures. Unfortunately, with all the money most people make, very little is saved. Over the course of your working life, you will likely earn enough to retire in the manner you would like. The key is to put a small portion of those earnings away for later. In the next few chapters, you'll see ways and places to put the money away and make it work for you.

AN EASY START TO SAVING

Saving money may seem like a daunting task, but it can be as easy as looking around your house or even your car. We have change jars in our house. There is a jar for the change I take out of my pocket or my wife from her purse. She also has a jar on top of the washing machine for that change I forget to take out of my pockets. It's an easy way to save. Those dimes or quarters may not seem like much when you look at them, but they add up quickly. Change jars are a great way to start. Go through the house and look for spare change. It could be on top of your dresser or in your car's floorboard. Put that change in a jar and you've begun your savings project. Now, don't leave the change in the jars or it won't be able to grow for you. You decide when you want to take your change and put it into a savings account. You might do this once a month or once a quarter. Roll the change up or take it to the grocery store where they have a change counting machine. If you really want to get excited about savings, each day put all your loose dollar bills in a jar that you can't see inside. Don't look inside that jar for one month. The dollars will add up quickly. It would not be hard to save $50.00 or more in that time. You can do a lot with $50.00, as you will see. Take that money and head to the bank. Those nickels, dimes, quarters and dollars will begin earning interest and growing for you.

FINDING WAYS TO SAVE

One of the largest expenditures for most families is at the grocery store. The U.S. Department of Agriculture did a 2007 study that showed the average American family of four spends between $6,700 and $13,200 annually on groceries. Wouldn't it be nice to be on the lower end of that average? Before you go to the store, make a list. Follow that list and look for bargain prices on your needed items. Some people can really save money by using coupons. It takes some effort and patience, but if you have the will, there is money to be saved. There are many great websites that offer coupons for free. Also watch for when your grocery store doubles or even triples coupon savings. Another big way to save on your grocery budget is with a freezer. You can purchase a good freezer for about $100. Use that freezer to stock up on meats, vegetables or even ice cream. These items can often be found for half price. For those with some room in the yard, a garden is another great way to save money. Growing your own vegetables saves money and can be a great place to teach children where their food comes from. Get excited about finding bargains and saving money.

You can save money on your power bills by turning off lights, adjusting your thermostat and unplugging unused electrical items. Save money on gasoline by combining trips. If you're headed to the grocery store, think of any other errands that you need to run and combine them into one trip. You'll save gas and thereby save money. There are many simple ways to save money.

BEGIN A FAMILY TRADITION

Now that you have a couple of ideas about saving money, get the family involved in finding others. If you have children, get them excited about saving money. Do they have a piggy bank or a savings account? Help them learn about saving while they are young. When they see their money adding up, they'll find their own ways to save money. Don't expect them to learn the importance of saving money in school. Most likely you didn't!

As we go forward, you will learn other ways to make your savings grow for you. The most important thing to remember as you begin is just to do it. Don't wait. Don't worry that it's not enough. You will see later that it is not the amount, but the time we start that makes the difference in our savings. By getting your savings habit started today you have taken the first step to improve your future!

CHAPTER TWO

PAY YOURSELF BEFORE
YOU PAY OTHERS

This chapter is one of the most important chapters in the book. You may have already heard of the concept of paying yourself first. It simply means that you must put money aside for yourself and your family before paying the mortgage, electric, grocery, or any other bills. The reason to pay yourself first is that if you don't, typically there is nothing left at the end of the month to put into savings. The payment to your future should be the most important bill you pay each month. I know personally, no one else is putting money in my bank account. It's up to me to do that. If you don't do it, how are you ever going to save anything? Well the sad truth is most people don't. Americans save less money annually than the citizens of any other industrialized country in the world. According to the 2006 U.S. CENSUS BUREAU report, Americans saved a -1% of their income. Yes, we saved a negative 1%. Things must change for us to have a better future for our children and for ourselves.

Most financial experts recommend we pay ourselves at least 10%-15% of our earnings per year. If you set aside 10%-15% of your income each month, before you see it, you cannot spend it on something you might not have needed in the first place. It is a fact of life in America that most people spend more than they earn. Many Americans are not living within their means. If we follow the example of our government, that is often living with a huge deficit. We can't continue to live in the red and expect to retire in the black. Too, often what happens is that we use a credit card to get back on track, which is the worst possible option. Then we end up paying interest on something we either didn't need or that we could have paid for out of our monthly budget. We have always wanted to keep up with the Jones'. Well we have, we are just as much in DEBT as they are!

THE BEST IDEA EVER

There are all kinds of ways to pay yourself first. Have you ever heard of a Christmas Club? Your local bank might have one that you can take advantage of. These accounts have been around for years. This is one way to pay yourself first. The bank has a planned amount for you to deposit every month. At Christmas time you will have saved enough to make your Christmas brighter and not have to worry about where the extra money will come from for your children or charities. A Christmas Club account could prevent you from putting your Christmas purchases on a credit card like so many do and then get deeper in debt. A monthly deposit of $25 or $50 could garner you $300 to $600 when Christmas rolls around. Consider this option if you struggle each holiday season or if you're still paying for little Tommy's bicycle for a year after he received it.

The Christmas Club is a great way to get in the habit of saving, but it's not a long-term solution. You need a savings plan focused on your retirement years. Your bank or credit union offers one option that many people don't even know about. It's called a **bank draft.** This option allows an automatic deduction be taken from your checking account each month or payday. In many cases, you can also have your employer automatically deduct an amount from your paycheck and have it go into your savings. This is called a payroll deduction. This is set up like the Christmas Club, but instead of going just into a savings account for holiday spending, the funds can go into just about any type of account that you desire. Your bank would make a withdrawal from your checking account and make a deposit in your savings, money market, IRA, or mutual fund. I found out about this by accident some 20 years ago and I am sure it was one of the most important things that I have ever learned about paying myself first. By using a bank draft to make a deposit to your savings, you can plan around your spending. Money we don't see we can't spend. You have probably realized by now that it is very difficult to have enough discipline to put money in your savings every time you cash your paycheck. With a bank draft set up it is much easier to save on a regular basis. You can set them up on any day of the month to move your money. To this day no bank person has ever mentioned to me that I could have this set up. It is so reassuring to know that I have money going into savings each month automatically. All I have to remember is to deduct it from my checking account just like any other bill.

A brief mention of budgeting, which to many of us is like the unpleasant task of dieting. By paying yourself first though, it will be a much easier task to make a budget. You will already have your savings taken care of first, instead of like many people that don't have any money left to save after paying bills. Then you can pay your bills and make other purchases and be aware of your spending habits. You will have a wonderful feeling of accomplishment in knowing that you are saving for your future.

A few sentences back there were a few terms you might not be familiar with. One term was called a mutual fund. These are very exciting and interesting accounts for our long-term savings goals. They will be discussed in chapter six. Another term was an IRA these are your tax savings investment accounts and can save you thousands in tax dollars. They will be covered in chapter seven. For now I want you to see and understand how to get your savings started and continued on a regular basis.

This is **STEP I** in developing a working plan that you can get excited about. By **paying yourself first** using a bank draft or a payroll deduction you are well on your way to making incredible changes in your future. Remember, it is not necessarily the amount you save, but when you start that is important.

CHAPTER THREE

HAVE AN EMERGENCY FUND

You now have your savings started and are paying yourself first each month. It's time now to set up an emergency fund. What is an emergency fund? It is just what it says, money to be used in case of an emergency. What happens when the car breaks down, the refrigerator stops keeping the drinks cold or the air conditioner goes out and it's 95 degrees outside? These things need to be repaired and it's not yet payday. What most people do in this case is get out the card and say CHARGE IT! Is that the right answer? It's not if you are trying to stay out of debt and trying to secure your future. Instead, we need a place to set some money aside, where it can earn interest, to use only in case of an emergency.

YOUR FINANCIAL CORNERSTONE

Having an emergency fund is the **cornerstone** of your financial building. Many experts recommend an emergency fund equal to between 3 and 6 months earnings. Of course, you can always have a bit more for a cushion, but 3-6 months would help out in case of an emergency. Let's say you bring home $1,500.00 a month in earnings. Your emergency fund should contain between $4,500 and $9,000. Some might say, WOW if I had that much I could RETIRE! That might sound like a lot of money to just have sitting there, but it's not, it's working for you. Your emergency fund will be in an interest bearing account. You could even take the interest at the end of the year and use it to take a small vacation or give you and your family some other reward for doing such a great job at saving. It would not hurt to take out the interest, because you only want this for an emergency fund not a retirement fund. If you were getting 5% interest on your $4,500, that's $225.00. That would pay for a weekend getaway and a nice dinner too. Do you see how much easier things can be with just a bit of information?

Now let's discuss where to put your emergency fund. Do not put it in your regular checking or savings account. Although it would be fine to have a savings account at another bank, maybe in a different town. Why should I go to the trouble of doing that you might ask? Well the reason is that this money needs to be a little more difficult to get out. You don't want it where every time you might run short of cash for a night out you can get to it. If you did, before long you might not have the money there for a real emergency. Another option would be to purchase CD's (Certificates of Deposits), but you might have to wait till the maturity date to get your money out without a penalty. Also, with CD's you might need a considerable amount of money just to get one started. One of the best places for your emergency fund is in a **money market** account. They are rather safe investment accounts, with no penalties any time you need to take money out. You can make regular monthly deposits that would fit in with your budget too. If you need some of the money it may take a few days to get it, which is exactly what you want from an emergency fund. It would refrain from a spur of the moment purchase but would be there if you really did need it. Your local bank or investment company should be able to help you set one up. A money market's rate of interest is fairly low though, partly because of its low risk. This doesn't make it great for long-term investing, but does make it a great place for your emergency fund. It will gain some interest with very little risk.

Without having an emergency fund can lead to all sorts of problems. We might be tempted to charge items on our credit cards, which would increase our debt. Or we might have to withdraw funds from our long-term savings to get us out of our emergency situation. Either of these should be avoided to make our money work harder for us.

Having an **emergency fund** is **STEP 2** and is the **cornerstone** to starting your financial plan, but is often overlooked or its importance is not emphasized enough. If we can remember one thing from here, is that to have money set aside for an emergency would bring us such peace of mind. What a nice feeling that would be!

CHAPTER FOUR

THE POWER OF COMPOUND INTEREST

Compound interest sounds like a boring banking concept, but in reality it can be your nest egg's best friend. All financial institutions know the importance of compound interest, but they don't always like to share their knowledge. Compound interest is one of the truly amazing facts of math. Most everyone knows that the money you deposit in your savings account earns an interest rate. What you might not realize is that as you continue to make deposits, every penny in your account earns interest. Yes, compound interest is where you earn interest on not just your deposits, but also the interest those deposits have earned. Compound interest makes our money work for us continuously 24 hours a day, 7 days a week, 365 days a year with no holidays or vacations. It grows while we work, sleep or even go fishing. As long as we have money in our account, that money is working for us and growing. Wouldn't it be nice to have a job like that, where you would be paid even when you were sleeping or playing? I have not found one like that yet! That is why it is so important to put compound interest to work for us so maybe down the road we will not have to work.

We all get bank statements and we can see where our money earned interest from the last statement. How nice is that? Even if we didn't add any to it, we still made money. In making our money work for us we must look at the interest rate we are getting. Most banks and insurance companies are usually paying us very little return for the use of our hard-earned dollars. Then they loan it out and make a much higher return. That is how they make money. Take a look at your credit card statement and you will see that they charge you 10-16% interest or even more. If you saved with the same bank as issued your credit card and they paid you 2-5%, they are earning 2-3 times what they are paying you, but you are the one that worked for that paycheck. We will talk about this more in chapter 6. For now though it is important to understand how you must fight for every point of interest you can get on YOUR money.

A SIMPLE RULE TO LEARN

In the money world there is a seldom discussed rule that is extremely important. It can be found in most financial books. It is very easy to understand and can help you with making saving and investing decisions. It is the **RULE of 72.** What in the world is that you might ask? I am not sure who figured this out, but maybe it was old Scrooge himself counting his money. The Rule of 72 is simply dividing an interest rate into 72 to get the number of years it would take money to double. For example, if you earn 5% on your money, divide 72 by 5, which equals 14.4. You now know how many years it will take your money to double. If you had $1,000.00 earning 5%, in just over14 years you would have $2,000.00. At 10% you would divide 72 by 10 for an answer of 7.2 years. So the same $1,000.00 would now be worth $2,000.00 in 7 years NOT 14 years.

Isn't that an amazing rule to know? Would you rather earn 5% or10% on your money? That is why it is so valuable to earn a few extra percentage points. It is a simple rule to keep in mind when we are looking to find a rate of interest on our savings.

INCREDIBLY   AMAZINGLY   EXCITING

Now it is time for you to really see something fantastic about the **POWER of COMPOUND INTEREST.** I certainly hope you can follow along, because this is truly amazing!

There were two young friends who had just graduated college and started their working careers. We will call them Joe and Tom for this example. They were both 21 years old. Joe was kind of a thrifty guy with his money and knew the value of saving. Tom just wanted to have a good time and spend his money. Joe knew about compound interest and how it could work for him. He started an investment account and figured that he could save approximately $38.50 a week, which is $2,000.00 a year, and not even miss it. He had a plan of doing this for ONLY 6 years to age 27 and then he would stop investing. That would be only $12,000.00 he had invested in those 6 years. Tom liked to party and spend his money on unnecessary purchases, so he didn't start saving anything until he was 27. At this time, he begins to save his $38.50 a week. Tom has waited to start when Joe has stopped his savings plan. Now this is what is incredible. Tom will save for the next 38 years to age 65. Joe had invested only $12,000, but Tom has had to invest $76,000. Who do you think will have the most money at age 65? In this example, they average a 12% return on their savings, which could be possible by using mutual funds (see chapter 6). Now this is what is INCREDIBLE. Assuming no withdrawals had been taken from either account and both are tax-sheltered accounts, Joe would end up with $1,510,253.00. Tom has done, ok too. In his account would be $1,529,942.00. THEY BOTH HAVE ALMOST THE SAME AMOUNT! Would you rather be Joe and invest $12,000 or Tom and have to invest 6 TIMES more?

	JOE			TOM	
Contributions	Savings	AGE	Contributions		Savings
$2,000	$2,240	21	-0-		-0-
$2,000	$4,749	22	-0-		-0-
$2,000	$7,559	23	-0-		-0-
$2,000	$10,706	24	-0-		-0-
$2,000	$14,230	25	-0-		-0-
$2,000	$18,178	26	-0-		-0-
-0-	$20,359	27	$2,000		$2,240
-0-	$22,803	28	$2,000		$4,749
-0-	$25,539	29	$2,000		$7,559
-0-	$28,603	30	$2,000		$10,706
-0-	$32,036	31	$2,000		$14,230
-0-	$35,880	32	$2,000		$18,178
-0-	$40,186	33	$2,000		$22,599
-0-	$45,008	34	$2,000		$27,551
-0-	$50,409	35	$2,000		$33,097
-0-	$56,458	36	$2,000		$39,309
-0-	$63,233	37	$2,000		$46,266
-0-	$70,821	38	$2,000		$54,058
-0-	$79,320	39	$2,000		$62,785
-0-	$88,838	40	$2,000		$72,559
-0-	$99,499	41	$2,000		$83,507
-0-	$111,438	42	$2,000		$95,767
-0-	$124,811	43	$2,000		$109,499
-0-	$139,788	44	$2,000		$124,879
-0-	$156,563	45	$2,000		$142,105
-0-	$175,351	46	$2,000		$161,397
-0-	$196,393	47	$2,000		$183,005
-0-	$219,960	48	$2,000		$207,206
-0-	$246,355	49	$2,000		$234,310
-0-	$275,917	50	$2,000		$264,668
-0-	$309,028	51	$2,000		$298,668
-0-	$346,111	52	$2,000		$336,748
-0-	$387,644	53	$2,000		$379,398
-0-	$434,161	54	$2,000		$427,166
-0-	$486,261	55	$2,000		$480,665
-0-	$544,612	56	$2,000		$540,585
-0-	$609,966	57	$2,000		$607,695
-0-	$683,162	58	$2,000		$682,859
-0-	$765,141	59	$2,000		$767,042
-0-	$856,958	60	$2,000		$861,327
-0-	$959,793	61	$2,000		$966,926
-0-	$1,074,968	62	$2,000		$1,085,197
-0-	$1,203,964	63	$2,000		$1,217,661
-0-	$1,348,440	64	$2,000		$1,366,020
-0-	$1,510,253	65	-0-		$1,529,942

How is that for a powerful message? JOE'S RETIREMENT IS MADE IN JUST 6 YEARS! He only saved for 6 YEARS! When I first saw this I did a double take. Maybe you did too. It still sticks in my head years after first seeing this. Perhaps you have a child or a friend that could benefit from this information. What a difference it could make in their future. If you want to have some fun, go and buy a compound interest calculator. They are relatively inexpensive. Or, if you have a computer you can find one on the internet. Back years ago I had to have one for my business and I would just put different amounts in and just see what they would grow to. Then you can see for yourself what a difference what compounding can do. What if we are not 21 though? Whatever your own situation is now, the principle is still the same. When money is saved and allowed to compound over time it can grow to great wealth for us all. I was 38 when I saw this and I'm still upset that no financial institution had ever showed this concept to me. It was only by being fortunate to have a friend introduce me to this, did I learn about the amazing POWER OF COMPOUND INTEREST.

CHAPTER FIVE

LET TIME BE ON YOUR SIDE

Getting older can be a wonderful part of life or a nightmare if you outlive your savings. When you're young and just starting out with new jobs and new families it seems like forever until retirement. That is what I thought when I was in my 20's. You began your first job and started making money. Now you could buy the things you'd always wanted, but couldn't afford before. What a great time of life? Then one day you wake up and wonder where has the time gone? High school seems like yesterday, but it was 10, 20 or 30 years ago. As the old saying goes, "Father time waits for no one."

In the last chapter you learned how you could use the power of compound interest and time to work for you. By using the TIME VALUE OF MONEY your money will have the chance to work. This is why it is so important to start as early as possible. It's not the amount you save, but rather the time the money has to grow. Remember Joe and Tom, the two 21-year-old guys? One started saving and the other waited just 6 years to start. They both ended up with about the same amount at retirement. One only put away $12,000 to make his money because he started early. Take a few minutes and go back and look closely at how each ones account grew. Even though Tom was continuing to invest his $2,000 each year it took him many years to catch up and pass Joe's account. When I first saw this example several years ago it was so amazing to me. Thinking back, no one showed or told me about the TIME VALUE OF MONEY and the compounding of interest. Who couldn't have saved a measly little $38.50 a week? Given this knowledge the choice would have been an easy one for me to do, those many years ago. The problem though is the lack of knowledge. When I see young people out today it gets me upset that they just don't know what this little idea could mean to them for their future. Time is FREE and everybody can take advantage of it.

WE CAN'T AFFORD TO WAIT

What if you're closer to me at age 55? It is never too late to get our saving habits started. You CAN teach old dogs new tricks especially when money is involved. We just have to save more, because time isn't as much a friend as it is for younger folks. We have to save sooner or later. Why not sooner?

Here is an example of the cost of waiting. If you could save around $38.50 a week, which is $2,000.00 a year. Invest it in a tax sheltered account and average an 8% return, this is what you could have. Pick the age closest to yours and see what it could grow to.

AGE	ACCOUNT VALUE
25	65 = $560,000
35	65 = $245,000
45	65 = $99,000
55	65 = $31,000

Can you see what a difference that time can make on our savings? From the age of 25 to 65 we could have $560,000, but by waiting just 10 years to age 35 we would have only $245,000. A difference of **$315,000**! Can we afford to wait any longer to get started? Just please remember it is not the amount that we save, but when we start that really makes the difference. This is the POWER of COMPOUND INTEREST and using time to work for you and your money. You can see for yourself the difference it makes to **let time be on your side.**

GROW A TREE AND NOT A GARDEN

I was in my car the other day and had a fantastic thought about your retirement plan. Have you ever planted a tree? Have you ever had a vegetable garden? Think of your savings as a tree you have just planted. The first few years it looks like your tree is growing very slowly. After many years though it begins to have a grand shape and offers us tremendous benefits to our home and family. Just like trees, savings accounts also take years for them to grow. A lot of the problems found in America today is that most folks tend to just grow a garden with their savings accounts. After using up the produce from the garden they have to start over the next year and every year. Many people have savings accounts that they build up and then take the money to buy something or use for a trip and then they have to start their savings over again. Their savings accounts constantly have to be started over and over just like the garden. So, for your money to work, you must grow a tree and not a garden. You have to save slow and consistently to make your money grow. Unless, your lucky to hit the lottery or receive a large inheritance you will have to save like the rest of us. Remember the old saying that "money doesn't grow on trees." Somebody had the right idea just had a few of the words wrong. It should say that **money does grow like trees**. Just imagine how great it will be when you retire to sit under your tree that you grew!!!

CHAPTER SIX

OWN YOUR MONEY, DON'T LOAN IT

It's time to talk about investments and let's try to keep it simple. Most folks think, like I did, that you have be some kind of financial wizard or very rich to buy or sell stocks. That is not the case. In fact there are ways for everyone to invest. A stock is what a company offers the public at a price so the company can raise money for equipment, expansion, etc. We see the news about the stock market almost every night. These days it all seems to be bad news. On the outside it appears to not be the place to put our money, but when we look at the history of the stock market we can see that it has been through a few difficult times and has always bounced back to new gains. You shouldn't think of using the stock market to get rich overnight, but rather to meet long-term financial goals. You should have goals of 10, 20, 30 or 40 years when using these investments then you can ride out the ups and downs that are inevitable in the stock market.

FREE ENTERPRISE SYSTEM AND YOU

When you go to the grocery store, there are thousands of products that you buy or are familiar with. Most of the companies that make these products offer stocks. They offer a chance as individuals to share in that company's growth. There is no crystal ball to see how a company will grow in the future, but you can look at the past to get an understanding. All the products you use everyday started out as just an idea. We have the freedom to take an idea and to build a company around that idea. That is what AMERICA is all about!!!

Now lets talk about how you can OWN a part of companies that you know. There are many investment companies that can help you. You see a few of them advertised on television. These are the middlemen between you and a company offering stock. You can pay them a set price to buy a share of stock for you. If you buy a stock then you can OWN part of that company. That is the free enterprise system in America.

Now for a minute let's look at LOANING your money. Banks, insurance companies and other financial institutions are necessary for our financial survival and they are an important part in your overall money plan. When you put money in the bank, they take that money and offer it back as a loan for a car, house or other need. They then charge an interest rate that is higher than the interest they will pay on your savings account. That is how they make money. They are NOT making money for you. You do need the banks, insurance companies or credit unions, but for things like an emergency fund, checking accounts, short-term savings, home loans, auto loans and protection against a financial loss. The problem though is that they are NOT the best place for your long-term investment goals.

Hopefully you will understand the big picture of OWNING vs. LOANING your savings dollars. It should be a basic part of your money management awareness. Most folks just are not told this information to make decisions on their own. It is not that difficult to understand once you learn the basics.

A GREAT PLACE TO SAVE

Now that we realize in order for us to get the best interest rate we can get, that we have to be **owners** and **not loaners**, where do we put it? A savings vehicle that has been around for a long time is something called a MUTUAL FUND. A mutual fund is where many people can invest a small amount of money and combine it into a pool of money and then an investment company can then buy shares of stocks in many companies. If 100 people put in $100 in an account, then that is $10,000 that a mutual fund can invest in stocks of different companies. If we tried to buy the same shares in companies it would be much more expensive. Mutual funds allow the individual to invest in any company, but with a much less savings dollar outlay. Many of us did not know there was such a place where if you have small amounts or large amounts of money we can invest in America. There are some mutual funds where you only have to invest a minimum of $50.00 a month.

Everyday the stock market is open, shares go up and down in price. Mutual funds are the same, because they are made up of many companies offering stock. The price for a share of a mutual fund is called the net asset value, (NAV) for short. Every weekday that the stock market is open, shares of mutual funds are traded the same as individual stocks of companies. You might have heard a phrase that says to BUY LOW AND SELL HIGH. Let's say you bought a stock at $10.00 a share and the next year it was valued at $12.00. Then you multiply $12.00 by the numbers of shares you own and this will give you the value. I learned a long time ago that accumulating shares is the way to increase your investment. That is how we make money in the stock market.

In every newspaper they have a money section where they have a list of mutual funds that are available for people to follow. Have you ever seen them and wondered what the heck is that? You are not alone. Before I found out about them I would just keep turning pages till I found the sports page. I didn't know that they were listed in there for me to take advantage of. Again the lack of knowledge raises its ugly head. In the paper there will be several columns beside each fund. They are prices each fund is selling for (nav) and annual return rate, load or no-load (load means the fund charges an up front sales commission percentage)—(no load means there is no sales commission charged), etc. We will not go into details, but there is a lot of good information in those columns.

WHY A MUTUAL FUND?

In Chapter 2 we talked about paying yourself before paying others. Mutual funds offer the perfect place to set up a long-term money account like an IRA. They can be put on a bank draft to invest on the same day of our choice each month. There are many benefits by using a mutual fund IRA and to set it up with a bank draft.

The FIRST is that we would have an automatic investment every month so we don't have to worry about taking the time to do it ourselves. We probably would not do it. Remember about paying a bill to yourself first. It is such an important key to have money set aside for your future. For me the bank draft has probably been the single most important key I have ever learned, but it all goes along with everything else.

The SECOND is a powerful concept called DOLLAR COST AVERAGING. We buy a share low and sell high to make money, right? The problem is when do we buy or when do we sell? With dollar cost averaging we don't have to time the market prices of mutual fund shares. When we put money in every month with our bank draft and the price for our fund is low then we are buying more shares. When our draft comes out and we buy and our fund price is high then we buy fewer shares. Over the long-term it has been proven that by investing on a regular basis using dollar cost averaging we will purchase more shares at a cheaper price than if we tried to time it ourselves. What you want to do is to accumulate as many shares that you can. When you decide to sell on down the road you multiply the number of shares by the share price to give you the value of your account.

A THIRD great advantage of using mutual funds is the diversification. What does that mean? It is a big word, but what it means is like the old saying "DON'T PUT ALL YOUR EGGS IN ONE BASKET." By using a mutual fund you are investing in many companies and not in just one as if you just bought stock in a single company. When you buy stock in one company you increase your risk on those dollars you invest. There is much less risk involved when you can spread your investments around in several companies. Also, mutual funds diversify in different sectors of the economy to help lower risk even more. For example a fund might invest in healthcare, oil and energy, technology, retail companies and other sectors. These are sectors and they give an investor the opportunity to shop around and look for a fund that is investing in a particular sector they are interested in. Let's say you work at a hospital, well you might would like to invest in a mutual fund that invests in healthcare companies. In that fund you would see names of familiar companies that you see everyday on your job. With the diversification of mutual funds, if one sector goes down, another will probably go up in price to equal out the overall performance of a fund. This is one of the nice benefits of mutual funds.

The FOURTH reason for using mutual funds is getting the knowledge and expertise of professional management working for you. In a mutual fund company each fund has its own fund managers. Their job is to do the research for you and to find the best companies that they believe will be profitable in the future. They analyze companies from inside and out before they make decisions on buying stocks in those companies and including them in your mutual fund portfolio. Sadly to say though, they are not always right with their stock picks. They use their experience and insight and research to make the best choices they can. No one has a crystal ball to predict the future. Here I must mention the fees for their services in managing our funds. Mutual fund companies will charge a percentage for each fund that you own. This fee is from the total assets that are managed under the fund. It could be from .5% to around 3% of the assets of each fund. It doesn't sound like very much, but many funds contain billions of dollars in assets. The more money they make for you the more they can make too. So they have a great incentive to do their best job at keeping our funds profitable. I have no problem with paying fund managers if they make me money. The mutual fund industry is very competitive with hundreds of funds for us to choose from. If we are not happy with a fund company we can always transfer our money to another fund company. A note here though that there could be a penalty fee charged if we withdraw our funds earlier than 6 months in most cases. Overall, it is hard to beat a mutual fund for your long-term investments.

Every mutual fund has what is called a prospectus. This is a brochure outlining all the details of the fund. It can be kind of technical at first glance, but it is important to understand the basic information in the prospectus. NEVER invest in a mutual fund without first reading a prospectus. Usually the first few paragraphs explain the investment objective and the risk category of the fund. It will detail all the fees associated with the fund. It also, may contain the current rate of return and the return since it started.

IS THERE ONE FOR YOU?

Mutual funds offer us at least the opportunity to get a higher return on our savings than any other investments. There are NO GUARANTEES when we invest in mutual funds or any stock related investments. You can lose interest as well as principle in a mutual fund, but only if you sell your shares. That one reason has scared off many an individual. Once people understand how they work and why we must find a place for our savings to make our money work for us they make so much sense. If you don't have at least a 5 year goal for your money you might want to just use a money market or a Certificate of Deposit(CD). account which is low risk, but also low return.

There are many mutual fund companies and each one of them has many separate funds for us to choose from. Their funds explain about the amount of risk and the potential of return of each one. A few keys to remember is that if your younger you want to look for more **aggressive** funds to save in and as we get older we need to look at having more **conservative** funds. Here is a little guide for you to follow. Count the number of years until you would like to retire and look to invest in those funds.

10 YEARS	=	CONSERVATIVE GROWTH FUND
20 YEARS	=	MODERATE GROWTH FUND
30 YEARS	=	AGGRESSIVE GROWTH FUND
40 YEARS	=	AGGRESSIVE GROWTH FUND

Every mutual fund company (investment company) has different funds for any person's situation. Investment companies make it easy to move from one fund to another and usually at no charge. This makes it convenient that as you get older you begin to shift more of your money to more conservative funds. Some investment companies now offer funds where they will automatically become more conservative the older you get and nearing your target retirement age. This is nice in that you don't have to discipline yourself to move your money, it is done for you. The more you understand how they work, the more you will benefit from them. When you go to town maybe then you can say that you own stock in McDonald's, Pepsi, Wal-Mart, and thousands of other companies you know.

We have been talking about the power of compound interest and for getting the best return for our savings dollars. Remember, about how important it is to get every point of interest we can on our savings dollar. Here is an example of what different rates will do to the growth of an investment:

Look closely at what just a few extra percentage points can make for our savings over time.

$100.00 a month saved at 3%, 5%,10%, and 12%
For   -   10 yrs   -   20yrs   -   30yrs   -   40 yrs

3%
10yrs = _____$14,000
20yrs = _____$33,000
30yrs = _____$59,000
40yrs = _____$93,000

5%
10yrs = _____$16,000
20yrs = _____$42,000
30yrs = _____$84,000
40yrs = _____$152,000

10%
10yrs = _____$21,000
20yrs = _____$76,000
30yrs = _____$217,000
40yrs = _____$584,000

12%
10yrs = _____$24,000
20yrs = _____$97,000
30yrs = _____$324,000
40yrs = _____$1,031,000

Are those some incredible numbers? There was a tremendous difference from earning 3% and 5% to earning 10% and 12%. Do you have an idea where you might could get 3-5% for your savings? You probably guessed, banks and insurance companies, and other financial institutions. Well you guessed right!! These are your **loaner** institutions. In order to make your money work harder for you is to be in an **ownership** situation. That is where you can have the greatest earning potential.

I want to challenge you to do a little more research on your on. Please go to your local library or the Internet and find out more about mutual funds. Remember though that any stock investment has NO GUARANTEE of a positive return for your money, mutual funds only offer the best potential for your long-term savings dollars. Do NOT INVEST in any stock related account without understanding them to your satisfaction. This is **STEP 3** in your learning of how to make your money work for you. Remember, to get your best return potential on your savings you must **OWN YOUR MONEY, DON'T LOAN IT!**

CHAPTER SEVEN

USE TAX SHELTERS

Would you like to get a BIGGER TAX REFUND check? Then hopefully you will like this chapter. If you are like me, tax issues are confusing and complicated. I just want to show you a few ideas about tax shelters that are available to almost everyone. Do you have an IRA? It stands for INDIVIDUAL RETIREMENT ACCOUNT. If not, then you are giving a lot of your money away to the government. An IRA is a tax shelter that can be used to save hundreds or thousands of dollars on taxes during your working years.

The highlights of an IRA are:

1. The dollars you put in could possibly be deducted from what you have earned for that year. Let's say you earned $20,000 in a year. If you saved $2,000 in an IRA you would only owe taxes on $18,000. You would owe less in taxes and would give you more for your savings.
2. Whatever money is in your IRA it earns interest tax deferred. Which means it can grow faster than if it was in a regular savings account. In a regular savings account at a bank you have to pay taxes on the interest you have earned.
3. Money that we have in our IRA would be taxed when we withdraw it at retirement, but at a lower tax rate than during our working years.
4. There is an early withdrawal penalty of 10% before age 591/2 for taking money out of an IRA. Also, you are taxed on that amount too. This is a positive in that it helps you to let compound interest

work for you. You have to leave it in and let it work for you. It is NOT a savings account it IS a RETIREMENT ACCOUNT!

5. There are now 2 kinds of IRA's, the Traditional and now the Roth IRA is gaining popularity. Each one has certain benefits for you to take advantage of.

6. The Roth IRA's biggest difference is that the money you put in grows TAX-FREE.

The government designed IRA's in 1974 to give employed individuals who didn't have a company retirement plan a place to save money and to offer us a tax break. They also offer a source of retirement income to help people to have more than just a little social security check, like my mom and probably somebody that you know who is struggling to get by. Sadly though, only 4 out of 10 households owns an IRA. We must SAVE for later and an IRA offers us a tremendous opportunity for our money to grow.

SHOW ME THE MONEY

Now for the answer to getting a BIGGER REFUND CHECK. One year I was looking over my tax return forms and found out that if I put in a few hundred dollars more in my IRA that I would get almost all of it back in my refund check. I was AMAZED! The money I put in my IRA was my money and not going to pay taxes. The reason was the deductibility benefit of my IRA and it reduced my taxable income amount by what I had deposited. Next time you get your IRS forms to fix, check to see what a few dollars more would do for your refund if you put them in your IRA. I bet you will like the difference it makes.

Now about that BIG refund check we get back. What do we do with it? Throw a big party, take a trip, down payment on a car, or just blow it. Most folks do the latter. They buy stuff they didn't really need to have. What if we got in the habit of taking HALF of it and put it in our IRA. We could make our money work TWICE for us. If we got back a $1000 refund check and we took $500 and put it in our IRA and did that for 10, 20, or 30 years at 10% rate of return. Let's see what it would be:

10 years   = $8,765

20 years = $31,500

30 years = $90,470

40 years = $243,425

That would be a nice little bonus to have and that is not counting what we already have in our IRA.

Here is another important note about your refund check. That big tax refund check we get back from the government is actually just an **overpayment** from us. We have overpaid what we needed to pay for taxes that year and the refund is just the government giving us our money back. Another thing about this refund is that the government has used our money all year and gave it back to us without it earning any interest for us. From the previous chapters you have seen what a few points of interest can do for our money. If you really get a large refund check you might want to talk to your company human resources person to refigure your tax status. If you get it changed where your company would take out fewer taxes then your payroll check would increase. Then you would have more dollars to invest without changing your current budget. It would take some discipline on your part to put that money back in your savings each month, but you can **do it.**

THE PERFECT ONE-TWO PUNCH

I hope you have seen the importance of an IRA and what it can do for your long-term goals. All banks offer IRA accounts and information on them. From what most experts say though is that banks can't offer the return that we need for this kind of account. Mutual funds in chapter six are the perfect match for an IRA account. Remember back in chapter four about the power of compound interest and how your money can grow over time. IRA's are for our long-term savings just like mutual funds should be used for. Just one other important note, your IRA is **not** your emergency fund or your regular savings account so DON'T TAKE THE MONEY OUT!

I encourage you to find out more about IRA's, but if you just know the basics and the importance in having one you would be better off. This is **STEP 4** for you to remember to combine an **IRA with a mutual fund** to minimize your taxes and to potentially maximize your long-term savings dollars.

CHAPTER EIGHT

SAVING MONEY ON INSURANCE

Please DO NOT skip over this chapter. If you are like me you hate to talk about insurance. It is a subject very few of us understand, so we tend to avoid it, but this is where your big dollar savings could come from.

WHY HAVE INSURANCE?

The purpose for insurance is to provide you and your family with financial protection in case of a large emergency. We all have insurance in some form or other, life, auto, homeowners, renters, health and many more, but yet we don't understand the fine print. As you will see what we don't know could be costing you hundreds of dollars a year in premiums. For small emergencies we can use our emergency fund, as we talked about in chapter 3, like a fender bender, or if we need to go to the doctor for an illness. For a larger emergency that we might have, we need to buy insurance. We pay a premium to an insurance company and they cover the risk for an amount of protection that we can afford. Many of us don't have enough in our savings to protect us in case of a catastrophic emergency, a house fire, car crash, health problems, or the event of a loss of life. These are all very disastrous situations, that we need to be prepared for if they should happen. To have adequate insurance protection for a large emergency is a very important part of our overall financial plan.

THREE RULES ABOUT INSURANCE

With just a few simple rules to follow you can save hundreds or thousands of dollars a year in premiums. Would you rather save more money or give it to your insurance company? Insurance is one of those necessary evils that we pay for, that we can't see or touch. As you will see what we don't know could be costing you hundreds of dollars a year in premiums. There are 3 simple rules that you need to know about when you buy insurance. These rules can save you a great deal of money. Here I want to list them and then explain each one.

1. Shop around to find the best deal
2. Buy the right life insurance
3. Raise your deductible

1. Shopping around speaks for itself. In America and with the free enterprise system we have competition, which helps us as consumers to find better products and prices. I get offers every week in the mail from credit card, car insurance, and life insurance companies wanting me to do business with them. That is the free enterprise system at work. With the computer and the Internet it is even easier today than ever before to shop around. We can just type in what we are looking for and in an instant we can find the information. My wife loves to go shopping like most ladies do and she shops from the convenience of our home on her computer. I must say, I love a good sale too. When looking for insurance premium savings, maybe think of it as a sale at your favorite store. When looking at prices and benefits, you do have to do a little comparison shopping though. Just make a list between what you have at present and the new offer and compare. For the most part, all insurance companies are about the same and are all regulated for their ability to pay claims. So don't be tempted by one you saw on TV or saw in a magazine. The companies that usually advertise are passing that cost down to the consumer in their premiums. Just look at what they can offer and the price they will charge you for that service to make your purchasing decision.

Maybe some of you have an agent loyalty issue. You have been with him or her for years and don't want to hurt their feelings. Well, how many payments have they made for you? You are looking out after your hard-earned dollars and trying to get the best product for your premium payments. Usually what happens though that I have seen is that the old agent will come back with a new offer when they find out that you have been shopping around. It has happened to me before and I ask them why didn't they tell me about it before? The reason comes down to the dollar they might be losing if you change companies. Enough said about this, but it could save you a lot of money by not being so loyal. Just please shop around.

2 Buy the right life insurance! What do you mean? From my personal experience and visiting with many clients over the years and from a lot of hours of research I discovered that most people own the wrong kind. With the support of many independent financial experts outside of the insurance industry, that also say most families purchase the wrong kind. Have you ever looked at your life insurance policies? If you are like me, they probably have been in a drawer since you received them. We are very uneducated about how life insurance works. Life insurance companies know that we don't like to talk much about life and death. The agent tells us that this is what we need and we are not sure what we are buying. I had bought a policy many years ago and I never even looked at it much less read and understood what was in those pages. It was only when a friend showed me things that really made a lot of sense that I learned what I had bought wasn't the best policy for me. I went to the library and did a little research and found out in AMAZEMENT that what most people buy is not the best policy for them! I found out that it was the best policy for the company and the agent to SELL, thus we have a serious conflict here. It was a conflict that could cost my family thousands of dollars!

FUNNY MONEY!!

Here are a few things that I found out after just a little research. Now I want to offer you a savings account. You put in a set amount of money each month. You earn interest on what is in this account, but if you need any, you must borrow your money and pay interest on what you borrowed or close out the account. How does that sound? What do you mean BORROW my money from my account? Whatever you take out you must pay interest on that amount. Another point about this account is that if you died, you would lose your savings! Yes your family would lose your savings! How many of these can I sell you? None of them, right! Well here is the shocker! Most people (maybe even you) right now in their homes have on average 1-3 of these accounts and don't even realize it. These accounts are your life insurance policies. There are many names for these so called cash value policies, whole life, universal life, variable life, paid up life, etc. They all combine a savings account with our protection coverage, because of this the insurance company keeps your savings and only pays the face amount. They also deduct any loan you might have taken out before any benefits are paid too. Sounds like a WIN WIN situation for the insurance company doesn't it?

All of this is written inside your own policy, but like millions of consumers it is not read or discussed in the sale. Many articles and books have been written about these kinds of policies and how they are NOT in our best interest to have them, but they are sold every day. My feeling is the lack of education on our part is the biggest reason we purchase an account like this. Most life insurance policies are sold with this combination of a savings feature and insurance protection. Insurance should be for protection only. They try to convince us that this is a forced savings for our future, and this combination has cost many Americans thousands of dollars. You do not have a savings account attached to your car, health, homeowners or any other kind of insurance, so why do they sell us on the idea of a savings account with our life insurance? My feeling is that it makes it easier to sell. Vultures have to eat too.

A BETTER ALTERNATIVE

What should we do then if we need life insurance protection? When I learned about this many years ago, everything I read said to buy TERM life insurance. I was never offered a comparison of term vs. whole life when I was sold my whole life policy. Life insurance should be a temporary need. It should be used to protect our family from the financial loss of a loved one. THAT IS ALL! Our biggest need for life insurance is when we have children that are financially dependent upon us. A good way to figure our need is to multiply our annual salary by our youngest child's age minus when they reach age 18. An example would be a child which is age 5 minus 18 would be 13 years. Multiply that by your annual income and that would be an adequate amount of protection to purchase. It would replace the loss of an income so the family could continue the same standard of living. When the children get older and go to college and begin their own families then our need should begin to DECLINE for life insurance, but our need should INCREASE for personal savings. Doesn't that make sense? Term life insurance fits in very well for those needs and you can buy a 10-20 or even 30 year policies. Another great thing is that it's much cheaper. You might be surprised at how inexpensive it is. For an example, a male that is in good health at age 35 could get a $250,000 non-smoker 20-year term life policy for around $300.00 a year. YES THAT IS RIGHT! For about $25.00 a month a family can have the protection they need if the unthinkable should happen. How much are you paying now? I would bet you are paying a lot more and have a lot less coverage. Find your policies and add up your premiums and also add up your coverage and see for yourself. When we get older, term insurance does get more expensive, but would you rather have a $100,000 insurance policy collecting dust or $100,000 in your IRA mutual fund account when you retire? By separating the insurance from your savings you can have the best of both worlds and be in control of it. Back in chapter six you learned that to get the best potential return on your savings that you need to be an owner and not a loaner. Well insurance companies would be considered a loaner and could never pay your best potential return. Remember to buy term life insurance and put those premium savings into your IRA mutual fund and you can save hundreds of dollars a year and build for your retirement.

3   Raise your deductible doesn't sound like much of a way to save, but it sure did me. What is a deductible? It is money that we have to pay before the insurance company begins to pay benefits on a claim. How can that be a good thing if we have to pay? Well we are taking on some of the risk from the insurance company if we have a claim. How often have you filed a claim? My guess would be that you haven't filed many claims. On our car and health and homeowners insurance there is a way that we can raise our deductible and that would **lower** our monthly premiums. By raising our deductible up just a few hundred dollars it could make a big difference in your annual premiums and you would have more to

save. If you ever do have a claim, your emergency fund would cover the extra expense of the deductible so that your benefits would then start. Your insurance is for a major need anyway and not for the little fender benders we sometimes could have.

Insurance buying is one of our least favorite things to do. We can't see it, smell it, or touch it until we need it. Then it becomes one of our most important purchases that we can make. There are many books and articles in your local library about buying the right insurance by many independent financial experts. I encourage you to read more about insurance and then you will become an educated consumer. Hopefully, you will be able to see through an agent's sale pitch and will know what questions to ask.

This is **STEP 5** and your final step to help you achieve your financial freedom. By raising your deductible you will now have more to go in your savings. Never combine insurance with a savings feature, it makes getting the protection you need very expensive. To get the maximum protection for your family for the least dollars is to **buy TERM life insurance**. To get the best deal on any insurance product, it will pay to shop around.

CHAPTER NINE

OUR FINANCIAL DISEASE

If you have watched any TV or read the newspapers you have heard of the credit crunch in America today. Mortgage, credit card and local banks are taking a closer look at customers credit history to make their lending decisions. They are tightening the reigns on who and how much a rate to charge for their loans. I don't want to sound too frightening, but there is a **financial disease** infecting our great country. It is our **personal debt** that many of hard working people are struggling with. Americans today are seriously in debt and this needs our attention if we are going to make a change for the better. We can all improve in this area of our finances with a few minor changes. It will be like the old saying "how do you eat an elephant, one bite at a time". Over time we all can reduce our debt to make our future brighter.

Over the last decade or so the banks have been getting fewer and fewer depositors. Because of this, banks must look elsewhere to increase their earnings. More and more banks are offering credit cards to offset this decline in deposits. This is their "cash cow" to make them more profitable. Personally I receive a few credit card offers in the mail about every week. These offers are made to be so tempting with low introductory rates and easy transfer of other balances to a lower rate. And also, I bet you have been PREAPPROVED for this new wonderful credit card. They make it sound like this is the answer to our money woes, but actually this can only lead to a larger personal debt. Don't fall for this credit trap, so just toss these new offers in the trash.

Back in chapter 3 we talked about having our emergency fund in place to help us if the fridge went out or if the car needed a repair. Since many Americans have overlooked this basic and most important financial fundamental, what they do is just say "CHARGE IT". The credit card has become many of our emergency funds for those unexpected emergencies that pop up from time to time. Then next month we receive our bill and look in bewilderment at our newfound debt. Many are already struggling to pay their minimum balance as it was before and now the balance has increased. What an endless and troubling circle of debt we are making. The best solution is to leave the credit cards at home and begin to build up your emergency fund. Only then can you begin to reduce your debt and start your wealth building for your future.

My thought on credit cards is that they can have a place in our finances if used properly. For people that travel on business or pleasure a credit card would almost be a necessity. They would need it for car rentals, motel reservations and airline tickets. For many thousands of Americans the use of a credit card is a daily occurrence. These are some of the best reasons to have a credit card. You might be able to think of a few other good reasons to have one. The problem I see is that we use them for groceries, buying presents, and spur of the moment items that we might not have needed if we had just thought for a minute or two.

If you decide to get a credit card, a good strategy might be to get a low available balance. Maybe use your monthly income as a guide to follow. For example if you earn $2,000 a month, set that up as your available balance. Then you will not tend to overspend if you do need to use it. If you ever maximize your card out, then that will tell you that you are overspending. Then you need to leave it at home and pay the balance before you can use it again. Two ways to to keep control of credit debt is to pay back more than the minimum or to pay it off each month. If you are now in some credit card debt it could be a good idea just to leave your card at home and pay for things with cash like the "good old days". The purpose here is not to send a negative message, but to just make people aware of the impact credit cards have made in all of our lives and to realize how much we use or abuse the privilege of having a credit card.

CREDIT VS DEBIT

Several years ago a new animal has been introduced onto the financial scene. It is called the DEBIT CARD. This card uses the funds that a person has in their checking or savings account to be drawn against for purchases. It has no interest rate attached to it, so it's use will not increase your debt like a regular credit card. Even though it doesn't have an interest rate with it we can still abuse this card also if we overspend. The debit card allows you to access funds if needed for purchases. Just remember to watch your spending and deduct it from your checking or savings account to avoid a fee. The debit card can be a handy and convenient addition sometimes instead of cash. As with any card we use, convenience must be associated with discipline.

I'm sure you have heard about how long it takes for water bottles and milk bottles to dissolve away in our landfills. I think the answer is never or 100 years. Well what are credit cards made from? Plastic, that is right! So just imagine your credit card balance as the landfill and that is about how long it will take for it to dissolve, too! If you have built up a sizable debt on your credit cards, you are not alone. There are many American families in the same floundering boat. If you need help, there are local agencies where you can get sound advice.

Unless you really need a card, my best advice would be to not have one. I hope this has been of benefit to you, just please don't get into credit card trouble. You will know when you are, it will be easy to spend, but hard to payoff. This financial disease called personal debt can be cured or avoided with a little discipline and a better spending awareness.

CHAPTER TEN

AN ATTITUDE ADJUSTMENT

It is so important for most Americans to realize that they need an attitude adjustment. Over the years many have become very dependent upon someone else to look after them. Many people believe that if they need it, they can depend on their city, state or even the federal government to assist them financially. That is not what the American Dream was supposed to be. Inside of each of us is the ability to make our own financial decisions and therefore make our own lives more secure. You do not need to be dependent upon anyone else to secure your future and the financial futures of your children and grandchildren. America remains the land of opportunity. In America, you can still start and own your own business, get a world class college education or work for a major corporation. It is up to you to make your own success both personally and financially.

FOUNDATION FOUNDATION FOUNDATION

In the real estate market you always hear the saying "location, location, location." I want you to learn a new saying, "foundation, foundation, foundation." You can build a secure financial life for yourself and future generations but you must build on a good foundation. Many of the wealthiest people in the world started at the bottom to achieve their financial success. If you believe in your abilities, you too can overcome many obstacles and achieve your goals.

There are 3 main reasons many people do not save enough money.

1   Procrastination   —Most people never get started
2   Lack of Knowledge   —Money matters are not taught to us in
                              schools
3   Just Don't Care   —Expect someone else to take care of them

Which category do you fall into? Since you had the interest to read this book then we know you are not in category 3. You've read this much so hopefully you've learned enough and you are no longer in category 2. As you've learned the basics in the book, perhaps you've already starting using them and are getting out of category 1.

Attitude is a big part of making a change for the better. You can't look at the past. You must look forward to your future. Not only can you learn from the things that you've read, but now you can share them with family and friends. Share with them how in Chapter 4 compound interest made a huge impact on Joe's and Tom's futures. Remember that Joe paid himself first for only 6 years. What would that mean to someone you know? My parents never learned the few principles that you have been shown. They worked hard all their lives sometimes working 2 jobs, just to retire barely above the poverty level. Unfortunately, when they retired, they had to live basically off their social security checks. Please don't look back 20 or 30 years from now and say "WOW where did the years go, why didn't I save more?" There are no more excuses now for you to wait any longer to get started on your road toward financial freedom.

YOUR NEW CAREER

Think back when you started a new job. Do you remember the feeling of insecurity about what was expected of you? You were not sure what to do and you had to be trained by someone else. Your confidence was very low until you could get adjusted to the new tasks that were required for the new job. The more you learned about your job and began doing it, your confidence began to grow. After a few days or weeks in training you became totally confident in your new job. Today, as you finish reading this book, you are in the training stage of your new financial job. Learn all you can and work every day to increase your financial confidence. It is up to you to retire when you **want to**, and not when you **have to**. Over the past few chapters, you've seen the basics and been given some tips to get started on your own financial journey. Now you can take these basics and build upon them. Your local library and the Internet are two great places to gather more detailed information about money management. Look on the APPENDIX II and III pages, you will see a list of the FIVE SIMPLE STEPS we've discussed throughout the book. You can tear out APPENDIX III and put it on the refrigerator for a quick glimpse reference guide to keep you focused on your financial goals. Use these steps to get your financial plan started and your goals can be reached. Read the steps, learn them and live them.

A THANK YOU

Thank you for your time in reading this most important book and please tell others about it if you found the information helpful. I would certainly love to hear from you if you have suggestions or comments about the book. You can email me at *mbfep@yahoo.com* and I wish you much success in your new financial career. Sincerely, K.C. Hobbs

P.S. Look for the MBFEP website coming soon. It will have facts and tips to help you gain more money awareness.

On the front cover you might have noticed the five green columns and wondered what they are? They represent the **five steps** you need to learn and also they represent Joe's saving account from chapter 4. Where he saved for only 6 years and over time it grew to an incredible amount for his retirement.

APPENDIX I

CHAPTER SUMMARIES

CHAPTER ONE   GET STARTED TODAY

Americans do not save enough money. If you don't want to retire in poverty, you must stop procrastinating and must start saving now. Everyone can find a few dollars each month to put in savings. Even small amounts saved are better than saving none. So put your quarters in a jar and GET STARTED.

"Saving money may seem like a daunting task, but it can be as easy as looking around your house or even your car. We have change jars in our house. There is a jar for the change I take out of my pocket or my wife from her purse. She also has a jar on top of the washing machine for that change I forget to take out of my pockets. It's an easy way to save. Those dimes, quarters and dollars may not seem like much when you look at them, but they add up quickly. Change jars are a great way to start."

CHAPTER TWO   PAY YOURSELF BEFORE
                                   YOU PAY OTHERS

For most people, it is very difficult to save money. The discipline is just not there. Monthly bills and unexpected needs use up every penny of your paycheck leaving nothing to set aside for savings. Paying yourself before you pay others is an easy to learn concept where the first money out of every paycheck goes toward your retirement. This chapter is **so important** because it reminds the reader that no one will put money away for their future if they don't. Using a payroll deduction or bank draft is an easy and automatic way to pay yourself first. You cannot spend the money that you do not see.

"Many of you have heard of paying yourself first. It simply means that you must put money aside for yourself and your family before paying the mortgage, electric, groceries, or any other bills. The reason to pay yourself first is that if you don't typically there is nothing left at the end of the month to put into savings. The payment to your future should be the most important bill you pay each month."

CHAPTER THREE   HAVE AN EMERGENCY FUND

An emergency fund is simply an account where you save money for a rainy day. It's not an easily accessible account, but one you can get to if a true need arises. The emergency fund is the **cornerstone** for your financial foundation. The emergency fund keeps you from taking money from your retirement account or using a credit card to pay for life's little headaches. It is recommended that an emergency fund is equal to between 3 and 6 months salary.

"One of the best places for your emergency fund is in a **money market** account. Most banks and mutual fund companies can set one up for you. They are rather safe investment accounts, with no penalties any time you take money out. Your local bank should be able to help you."

CHAPTER FOUR   THE POWER OF COMPOUND INTEREST

Compound Interest is truly one of the amazing facts of finance. It is the ability of our money to grow given an interest rate and using time. This is where you see how even small amounts can become fortunes when left to grow.

"Most everyone knows that the money you deposit in your savings account earns an interest rate. What you might not realize is that as you continue to make deposits, every penny in your account earns interest. Yes, compound interest is where you earn interest on not just your deposits, but also the interest those deposits have earned. Compound interest makes our money work for us continuously 24 hours a day, 7 days a week, 365 days a year with no holidays or vacations. It grows while we work, sleep or even go fishing. As long as we have money in our account, that money is working for us and growing."

CHAPTER FIVE   LET TIME BE ON YOUR SIDE

This chapter goes along with the use of compound interest to grow wealth. Whatever the age of the individual, time can be on your side, but you need to start now. Find out what it could cost us to wait. "Time waits for no man" is an old saying and how true it is in finances.

"By using the TIME VALUE OF MONEY your money will have the chance to work. This is why you need to start as early as possible. It's not the amount you save, but rather the time the money has to grow. Remember Joe and Tom, the two 21-year-old guys? One started saving and the other waited just 6 years to start. They both ended up with over a million dollars at retirement. One only put away $12,000 to make his money because he started early."

CHAPTER SIX   OWN YOUR MONEY, DON'T LOAN IT

For money to work the hardest for us we must invest where it can get the best earning potential. When you put your money in a bank or insurance company, they pay a low rate for the use of your money. They then loan it out and get a higher return for them. Mutual funds offer us the best way to get the best return.

"Most folks think, like I did, that you have be some kind of financial wizard or very rich to buy or sell stocks. That is not the case. In fact there are ways for everyone to invest."

CHAPTER SEVEN   USE TAX SHELTERS

IRA's have been around since 1974, but many AMERICANS are still not taking advantage of them. Money saved with in an IRA account is sheltered from taxes so it can grow faster than if it was in a regular savings account. If your not using an IRA, it could cost you thousands of retirement dollars.

"Do you have an IRA? It stands for INDIVIDUAL RETIREMENT ACCOUNT. If not then you are giving a lot of your money to the government. An IRA is a tax shelter that can be used to save hundreds or thousands of dollars on taxes during your working years."

CHAPTER EIGHT   SAVE MONEY ON INSURANCE

You probably have several types of insurance. What you don't know could cost you hundreds or thousands of your hard-earned dollars. Always buy TERM life insurance. It offers the most protection for the least premium. Never combine savings with life insurance, it makes getting enough protection too expensive. Raise your deductible on other kinds of insurance like auto and health to save on annual premiums. Always shop around to find the best deal.

"Insurance should be for protection only. You do not have a savings account attached to your car, health, homeowners or any other kind of insurance, so why do they sell us on the idea of a savings account with our life insurance? My feeling is that it makes it easier to sell. Vultures have to eat too."

CHAPTER NINE   OUR FINANCIAL DISEASE

It's no big news story that most Americans use too much credit. Every week, you probably receive multiple credit card offers. Banks make it so easy to apply and receive a card. There is a place for a card, for business or a vacation. I recommend shopping around for the lowest possible rate and a low credit balance. The lower balance helps you to not abuse your credit card.

"I'm sure you have heard about how long it takes for plastic water and milk bottles to dissolve away in our landfills. I think the answer is never or 100 years. Well what are credit cards made from? Plastic, that is right! So just imagine your credit card balance as the landfill and that is about how long it will take for it to dissolve, too!

Unless you really need a card, my best advice would be to not have one. I hope this has been of benefit to you, just please don't get into credit card trouble. You will know when you are, it will be easy to spend, but hard to payoff. This financial disease called personal debt can be cured or avoided with a little discipline and a better spending awareness."

CHAPTER TEN   AN ATTITUDE ADJUSTMENT

Americans have become lazy when it comes to finances. Many people expect someone else to take care of them. Today is the day you can stop that type thinking. It's time to grab the bull by the horns and gain the knowledge necessary to become self-sufficient in your finances. This change in attitude can help not only your personal finances, but the attitude your children approach their own money management and their financial futures.

"It is so important for us as Americans to realize that we need an attitude adjustment. Over the years we have become very dependent upon someone else to look after us. We think that the government, state or our city will help us financially if we need it. That is not what the American Dream was supposed to be."

APPENDIX II

FIVE SIMPLE STEPS WE MUST DO

1   PAY YOURSELF FIRST

Even small amounts can add up over time. Pay yourself first by using a **bank draft** or a **payroll deduction** and save 10-15% of your income. Make this your most important bill.

2   HAVE AN EMERGENCY FUND

This is the **cornerstone** to your savings future. You need this in place to cover unforeseen emergencies that might arise. What a great feeling that would be to know that you could weather any financial storm.

3   INVEST IN MUTUAL FUNDS FOR RETIREMENT

Mutual funds offer us the best interest return potential over time even though they are not guaranteed. Remember to **be an owner and not a loaner** for your best return potential.

4   USE AN IRA FOR TAX SAVINGS

To get maximum tax savings on our money we must have an IRA. By combining an **IRA with a mutual fund** you can increase you earning power tremendously.

5   BUY TERM LIFE INSURANCE

Term life insurance offers the most protection for the least premium. **Never combine insurance with savings**. It makes getting the protection we need far too expensive. Look for 10-20 or 30 year term plans to cover the loss of an income depending on the age of the children.

(refrigerator tear out page)

APPENDIX III

FIVE SIMPLE STEPS WE MUST DO

1 PAY YOURSELF FIRST

Even small amounts can add up over time. Pay yourself first by using a **bank draft** or a **payroll deduction** and save 10-15% of your income. Make this your most important bill.

2 HAVE AN EMERGENCY FUND

This is the **cornerstone** to your savings future. You need this in place to cover unforeseen emergencies that might arise. What a great feeling that would be to know that you could weather any financial storm.

3 INVEST IN MUTUAL FUNDS FOR RETIREMENT

Mutual funds offer us the best interest return potential over time even though they are not guaranteed. Remember to **be an owner and not a loaner** for your best return potential.

4 USE AN IRA FOR TAX SAVINGS

To get maximum tax savings on our money we must have an IRA. By combining an **IRA with a mutual fund** you can increase you earning power tremendously.

5 BUY TERM LIFE INSURANCE

Term life insurance offers the most protection for the least premium. **Never combine insurance with savings**, it makes getting the protection we need far too expensive. Look for 10 or 20-year term plans to cover the loss of an income. Raise deductibles to save on annual premiums.

70235NOTES

NOTES

APPENDIX IV
ORDER COUPON PAGES

To order additional copies of this book,
MONEY BASIC$ FOR EVERYDAY PEOPLE
Xlibris Corporation
1-888-795-4274
www.Xlibris.com
Orders@Xlibris.com
ID 70235

To order additional copies of this book,
MONEY BASIC$ FOR EVERYDAY PEOPLE
Xlibris Corporation
1-888-795-4274
www.Xlibris.com
Orders@Xlibris.com
ID 70235

To order additional copies of this book,
MONEY BASIC$ FOR EVERYDAY PEOPLE
Xlibris Corporation
1-888-795-4274
www.Xlibris.com
Orders@Xlibris.com
ID 70235

To order additional copies of this book,
MONEY BASIC$ FOR EVERYDAY PEOPLE
Xlibris Corporation
1-888-795-4274
www.Xlibris.com
Orders@Xlibris.com
ID 70235

To order additional copies of this book,
MONEY BASIC$ FOR EVERYDAY PEOPLE
Xlibris Corporation
1-888-795-4274
www.Xlibris.com
Orders@Xlibris.com
ID 70235

To order additional copies of this book,
MONEY BASIC$ FOR EVERYDAY PEOPLE
Xlibris Corporation
1-888-795-4274
www.Xlibris.com
Orders@Xlibris.com
ID 70235

To order additional copies of this book,
MONEY BASIC$ FOR EVERYDAY PEOPLE
Xlibris Corporation
1-888-795-4274
www.Xlibris.com
Orders@Xlibris.com
ID 70235

To order additional copies of this book,
MONEY BASIC$ FOR EVERYDAY PEOPLE
Xlibris Corporation
1-888-795-4274
www.Xlibris.com
Orders@Xlibris.com
ID 70235

To order additional copies of this book,
MONEY BASIC$ FOR EVERYDAY PEOPLE
Xlibris Corporation
1-888-795-4274
www.Xlibris.com
Orders@Xlibris.com
ID 70235

To order additional copies of this book,
MONEY BASIC$ FOR EVERYDAY PEOPLE
Xlibris Corporation
1-888-795-4274
www.Xlibris.com
Orders@Xlibris.com
ID 70235

To order additional copies of this book,
MONEY BASIC$ FOR EVERYDAY PEOPLE
Xlibris Corporation
1-888-795-4274
www.Xlibris.com
Orders@Xlibris.com
ID 70235

To order additional copies of this book,
MONEY BASIC$ FOR EVERYDAY PEOPLE
Xlibris Corporation
1-888-795-4274
www.Xlibris.com
Orders@Xlibris.com
ID 70235

To order additional copies of this book,
MONEY BASIC$ FOR EVERYDAY PEOPLE
Xlibris Corporation
1-888-795-4274
www.Xlibris.com
Orders@Xlibris.com
ID 70235

To order additional copies of this book,
MONEY BASIC$ FOR EVERYDAY PEOPLE
Xlibris Corporation
1-888-795-4274
www.Xlibris.com
Orders@Xlibris.com
ID 70235

To order additional copies of this book,
MONEY BASIC$ FOR EVERYDAY PEOPLE
Xlibris Corporation
1-888-795-4274
www.Xlibris.com
Orders@Xlibris.com
ID 70235

To order additional copies of this book,
MONEY BASIC$ FOR EVERYDAY PEOPLE
Xlibris Corporation
1-888-795-4274
www.Xlibris.com
Orders@Xlibris.com
ID 70235

To order additional copies of this book,
MONEY BASIC$ FOR EVERYDAY PEOPLE
Xlibris Corporation
1-888-795-4274
www.Xlibris.com
Orders@Xlibris.com
ID 70235

To order additional copies of this book,
MONEY BASIC$ FOR EVERYDAY PEOPLE
Xlibris Corporation
1-888-795-4274
www.Xlibris.com
Orders@Xlibris.com
ID 70235

To order additional copies of this book,
MONEY BASIC$ FOR EVERYDAY PEOPLE
Xlibris Corporation
1-888-795-4274
www.Xlibris.com
Orders@Xlibris.com
ID 70235

To order additional copies of this book,
MONEY BASIC$ FOR EVERYDAY PEOPLE
Xlibris Corporation
1-888-795-4274
www.Xlibris.com
Orders@Xlibris.com
ID 70235

www.ingramcontent.com/pod-product-compliance
Lightning Source LLC
Chambersburg PA
CBHW021908170526
45157CB00005B/2021